Sermon on a Perfect Spring Day

Sermon on a Perfect Spring Day

Poems

Philip Bryant

Minnesota Voices Project Number 85

New Rivers Press 1998

First Edition
Manufactured in the United States of America
   for New Rivers Press
Library of Congress Catalog Card Number: 97-69734
ISBN: 0-89823-185-x
Edited by Mark Vinz
Copyedited by Joanne Fish
Cover art by Norbert Blei
Book design and typesetting by Steven Canine

New Rivers Press is a nonprofit literary press dedicated to
publishing the very best emerging writers in our region,
nation, and world.

The publication of *Sermon on a Perfect Spring Day* has
been made possible by generous grants from the Jerome
Foundation; the Minnesota State Arts Board (through an
appropriation by the Minnesota Legislature); the North
Dakota Council on the Arts; Target Stores, Dayton's, and
Mervyn's by the Dayton Hudson Foundation; and the
James R. Thorpe Foundation.

Additional support has been provided by the Elmer L.
and Eleanor J. Andersen Foundation, the Beim Foundation,
the General Mills Foundation, Liberty State Bank, the
McKnight Foundation, the Star Tribune/Cowles Media
Company, and the contributing members of New Rivers
Press.

New Rivers Press
420 North 5th Street, Suite 910
Minneapolis, MN 55401

www.mtn.org/newrivpr

For Renée

Contents

Acknowledgments

The author wishes to extend special thanks and appreciation to the following people for their help, support, and spirit over the years: James and Alyce Bryant (in memory), Lee J. Kingsmill, Ann Sullivan, John Rezmerski, Elmer Suderman, Lawrence Owen, Rodney Davis, Michael S. Harper, Bill Holm, Norbert Blei, Janine Marie Genelin, and the Minnesota State Arts Board.

Some of the poems in this collection have appeared in the following publications: *Blue Island* (Chapbook), published by Cross+Roads Press, Ellison Bay, WI; *Indiana Review*; *The Iowa Review*; *Mankato Poetry Review*; *Midwest Poetry Review*; *Obsidian II*; and *Black Literature in Review*.

Sermon on a Perfect Spring Day

"Open your minds and hearts
to God," the preacher said
in closing.

"Gladiolus," someone shouted
from the back pews.

"Gladiolus!"

1959, Loomis Avenue

The intimate smell that belongs
to the poor and nobody else
drifts out into the streets
at dusk.
My cousin and I
play in the yard
where I soon notice there
is no grass, just a
clean dirt patch leading
to the alley. Our voices
reverberate among the other
sounds of the street as we kick
beer cans and throw shreds
of broken pop bottles through
the humid August air.
It is 1959. There are no
cries of bloody murder yet,
no guns or sirens or
ghostlike figures
dragging the street for a corpse to fix,
only the sound of children's
voices playing in
the growing rubble,
the smell of cooking collards
and fried chicken and the
Naugahyde-laminated family
Bible propped on the reading
table in the living room.
My cousin—with beautifully braided
pigtails and clean cotton blouse
so stiffly starched white on Sundays
she almost cracks as she moves—
jumps double dutch on the
sidewalk, her small brown legs turn
perfect loops over the old laundry ropes

in the almost darkness.
She looks to me as if she
were suspended in air,
and I imagine her ascending to
heaven to receive Jesus,
like the preacher on the radio said
late that Sunday night: "He will
receive us as little children."
As the streetlights come on
and the sky fades into turquoise blue,
a few ominous stars appear on the horizon,
and I hear my aunt's slow, solid-hipped
southern drawl
through the darkness
calling us home.

Some Notes on My Origins

When I first heard "Just a Gigolo" played by Thelonious Monk, I was seven or eight and still could see under the hems of skirts but was no longer allowed to hide under them. The sound always came from above, which I attributed to being some kind of heaven, not in the Christian sense, but in the Monk sense, a bebop heaven, where my dad was Jesus and wore a goatee, Basque beret, read Shaw and Hemingway and talked of substitute cords of fifths and sevenths.

I first discovered the Negro Church around eleven. Everything was mahogany. The old mahogany pews moaned. The old mahogany women moaned even louder:

> *Take me up to Jesus*
> *So I can see His face.*
> *Take me up to Jesus*
> *So He can know my name.*

They sang mahogany spirituals, mahogany gospels, and prayed mahogany prayers. You can imagine with all this mahogany sweating and moaning on a hot summer morning, what church smelled like — we were higher than kites. "*Happy*," as they would say. Yes, the black church is really the mahogany church. My church was not stained in the blood of Jesus but stained with a mahogany undercoat. Jesus was still white then, but brown rivulets of very good mahogany wood stain were encroaching in on him. Still white, he sadly hung there on the cross.

I'll end with "Little Rootie Tootie," which is another Monk tune about the evolution of the species. In my neighborhood on the Southside, we had every species imaginable. They were all on the lam, every single rare animal, plant, and bird you could think of. They heard the Southside was a good place to lay low — *be cool.* No one came looking for you or paid attention to what went on, especially after dark, unless it was a heinous murder, a big fire that made fourteen children homeless in the middle of February or some policy queen was busted. In between those happenings it was a sanctuary and developed a live and let live atmosphere. It was an unofficial wildlife preserve. Darwin's

Beagle could have dropped anchor right on 35th and Indiana and written *Origin of the Species* while he partook of some good blues music at the Checkerboard and barbeque ribs at Lem's. So came "Little Rootie Tootie" and the origin of all life from one common ancestor. As my uncle would have said, "Yeah, the original man? I knew the nigger; he stayed four doors down from where Aunt Janey lived when she first came up from Mississippi."

Some Streets in Chicago

SOUTH STATE STREET

The far western outskirts, a barrier or border like the Great Wall of China. To the west, the teaming hordes, barbarians from the cotton patches and corn fields of the deep South that you shared a classroom with and marveled at their broken rain gutter speech, wild, violent mood swings and the run-down, dilapidated houses they squeezed into after school.

WABASH

The first tree-lined street after State:

It looked like my street but bordered State and that made it less so. No apartments, small bungalows hidden in thick elms and maples. To the north, home of the infamous "Juicy," 250 pounds already at eleven; would do anything you wanted in her basement, so it was rumored. Once I got up the nerve to ride my bike over there, to try my luck. There's her mother, 450 pounds, straining the plastic fabric of a lawn chair on the front porch. "No she can't play, honey, she gone to Mississippi for the summer to be with her aunt and uncle." I remember turning my bike and peddling as hard as I could, my face still flushed and hot.

MICHIGAN

It was a street always dark from the very beginning, even in the middle of the day on a sunny hot cloudless afternoon in July. Older people lived on Michigan. You never saw them—only in the evening coming home from work or cutting or sprinkling the grass. Only a few had children, and they were quiet and played by themselves.

INDIANA

The cleanest, most "siditty" well-kept block in the area—no trees, solid brick bungalows, and fortified two flats—stark, cold: that upward and onward look. It was included with "going around the block" on your bike. One year a boy that I knew only vaguely was cut into by a shotgun blast while trying to open his front door. It was rumored that he was an "example" for us, the intimidated, because he didn't join the 71st Street Bowery Boys.

PRAIRIE

My seed street: grass, grass, grass! When I was growing up, tall elms arched over the wide avenue. In the fall these leaves would be burned in piles along the curb. There was also white, numbing bareness in winter. From 74th and Prairie you could hear the distant bells of St. Ignatius and see the sea green steeple of the Lutheran church illuminated by flashes of lightning during a summer storm.

CALUMET

Always the most disheveled looking: landed gentry fallen on hard times. Kids who lived just a yard's length away from me growing up with all the advantages and creative comforts of home and for all my life I didn't know their names nor did they mine. Yet, they miraculously turned out to be Jesse James, John Dillinger, and Ma Barker.

SOUTH PARKWAY (OR MARTIN LUTHER KING JR. DRIVE)

Legendary! The yellow brick road. The Trail of Tears people poured out and had an impromptu parade/celebration after the Louis/Baer fight. Brought my mother home from work as well as took her away. We'd wait at 74th for the No. 3 South Park bus to pull up, almost empty, and see her small, delicate frame get off the bus. It was a joyous reunion straight out of a movie, yet a movie could never get it right. They never do.

Independence Day 1960

Around the dawn of time,
before black people were
ever conceived of or invented,
a thousand fires would
be lit on the Southside of Chicago.
Smoke rose over the flag-draped
streets and rooftops. Everything from
early morning reveille to the "Star Spangled Banner"
was sung by Dinah Washington or Johnny Mathis.
The summer heat and humidity festered
in the wide dark Buicks and Cadillacs that
began to roll up the streets in late afternoon.
Wooden horses appeared, blocking the intersections.
Pork ribs and chicken legs slowly simmered on the
grill. Bottles of Bud and Miller
popped and popped and popped.
So too, laughter and phonographs turned up
to Jimmy Smith's "Sermon," Cannonball's
"Jive Samba" and "Work Song."
The people sweltered in the
backyards, kicked up a fuss over
badminton, softball, or croquet.
Later that evening,
punctuated by the steady popping
of sparklers and Roman candles
the flag with just forty-seven stars hung listlessly
in the humid night air outside
our brick three flat.
The adults sipped highballs,
spoke in low tones so my cousins
could not hear "grown folk's talk"
as they asked for another Dreamsicle—
"Isn't that your fifth already today?"
We'd swear it was "just our fourth tonight, Janey."
"Don't play me for no fool now,"
and Janey would mask her laughter in a mock serious tone.

"You better go ask your momma.
She's the one who's got to put up with you
running to the bathroom all night."
As all this happened
on the Fourth of July,
our own Independence Day, 1960.

The Forbidden Fruit

The first person
who ever called
me a nigger
was Jasper Magee,
my best pal,
who was seven years old
and two shades darker than me.
He never knew
what a nigger was.
Neither did I—
even though we laughed guiltily
after he'd said it again
the way he heard the older boys say it
on the playground.
It tasted a little
like forbidden fruit
to our young mouths,
the kind of words our parents
spoke in low whispers
long after we went to bed,
or the way Jasper let it
slip from his mouth
once more in the deserted alleyway
when it was almost dark.
It still had the taste and look
of that sweet red fruit
just bitten into.

Portrait of My Father

The first time I felt his hands lifting me up like a gust of wind taking a small scrap of paper to wind, I thought it was some obdurate God. The great unseen. Suddenly floating, I was above it all. I could fathom his dark hands lifting me to the cradle—thinking I was asleep. Yet, one eye cocked in a two-year-old imagination, I was suddenly weightless, drifting and gliding ever since. Only now I know who propelled me up so mysteriously that day. I remember him in his chair surrounded with books—"a man's home is his castle"—those thick bound texts, the bricks and walls, the drawbridge drawn up, a deep moat silently flowing and glistening below kept out the hard facts of the age we lived in whizzing by the apartment window. In a flurry of craven upward mobility and progress of the race, everything was a tool, a weapon to forge ahead to the future. My father would claim his glass of suds and secretly connect the ages together in his cloistered head full of Bird, Monk, Diz, and Trane: a rickety vespers, a veritable hum of living in the dark ages. He, with his rounded, fair face, mustache and goatee, ragged moth-eaten army sweater and baggy chino pants, blue lacquer breath and ever-present can of Schlitz Malt Liquor, concocted his holy order of one: a singular monk sharing a monastery with his family. I could never pierce the vow of silence except to talk books, jazz, art, or sports. He would go deep into the vaults, pull a record and say, "Listen to this." Gene Ammons's, "Canadian Sunrise," which he'd marked on the record sleeve, "**** Stars James Bryant." Now I can understand the sudden rages, the fear-laced thrashing, cajoling and senseless, a lever against his own failings, mirrored in his blood and looking and acting like him more each day. He never saw that his weaknesses were his strengths; his foibles, the gifts he imparted. He didn't believe it nor did he feel they held anything for him. So now I can see him plainly on that hot sultry day in early June walking down the street with his workman's satchel filled with aprons and gloves, dressed in boots and overalls. He will go inside, pull a Schlitz, pop on Sonny Stitt as the evening settles down before him; he recounts the ages in his head as the music plays around him. Now, I'm not sure what lifted me into my crib that day so gently from the corner where I slept. What lifts any son toward his father—each a seed of his own lonely hour—pulling farther apart yet closer still; the sense of hands lifting, at other times just gliding along with it, not knowing who is behind; the actual lifting up: so steady, so nameless and unknown.

Moses and the Ten Commandments

He held the
record album high
over his head
like Moses
coming down
from Mount Sinai
with the Ten Commandments:
"Perfect, I tell you, perfect."
It was the new Miles Davis
album, *Kind of Blue*—
with John Coltrane
and Cannonball Adderley,
and he stood there
beside the hi-fi system
in just his white
terry cloth robe,
his dark brown face shining
in the morning sunlight,
striking that beautiful
biblical pose.
Suddenly I believed him
and even now
I still do.

Passover Hamburgers

The hamburgers
were greasy and overdone.
The buns burnt almost black
and hard for us to hold
in our small hands,
but we ate them anyway
and as we swallowed hard
they'd stick in our throats
sometimes causing us to choke
in silence.
On the other hand,
my father looked up
from the stove
and for one of the few
times I can remember
he truly looked happy
and content.
We signaled our false approval
with two thumbs up
and ate his singular
and lone offering
of love
with the grim determination
of grateful supplicants
eating
bitter herbs.

Father's Bouquet

My dad not only
burned the imaginary
midnight oil
but drank it too.
And it burned inside
of him throughout
all his days until they
turned to
black cinders.
Each one
became a flower in the bouquet
that he bequeathed
to me, his son,
to plant beside
his grave
one day,
or maybe when
they got old and dried up
to simply
throw away.

New Year's 1965 at Aunt Janey's

A hog's head
filled with
black-eyed peas
and okra,
cornbread, chit'lin's
and coleslaw—
next to the traditional turkey,
dressing, and cranberry sauce.
My grandmother from the South sits and talks
lovingly about Tony Bennett, Perry Como,
and Andy Williams: "those Eye-*talians* sure can sing."
She watches Lawrence Welk religiously every Saturday
night, right before "Half GunWill Travel" and "Gunsmoke."
Someone puts on a Bobby Blue Bland record
and kicks up her heels. "Pour me
another Johnnie
Walker Red, please."
"Ho, Ho, what's that?"
Someone brought a batch of
fried hog maws in out of the cold. "Who's gonna eat those?"
"Is that Aunt Janey lookin' as big as a house?"
"*Girl*, you oughta be shot."

Dancing with Aunt Janey

Aunt Janey, in a tight black dress on New Year's Day,
was doing the shimmy and dancing
the black bottom
as her enormous buttocks whipped about
like the black and starless night sky
in late, windblown March.
I was ashamed that I
wanted her like a man would
want a woman a moment
after first laying eyes on her.
I was too young to know
the train whistle guitar
that blew from way down under
from long distances away
could be heard even by me.
"Don't ever play on them tracks, boy,
because you might look up
and not see it coming
'til it's too late."
Aunt Janey would say,
"Come on here boy, show me
your stuff." She would laugh
drunkenly and I would
pretend to shimmy and reel,
but stumble into the
warm blackness of her dress—
sweaty and strong with her sweet odor
mixed with cigarettes and scotch.
She would hold me against
her great, heavy breast
and I could almost
feel her heart beating,
keeping perfect time
with mine as Miles
played the mute and
sputtered "Billy Boy" all over the floor

as now her glistening sweat
and laughter cooled
and anointed my brow.

Card Sharks

They all sat around
during the lull
quietly looking at their
hands—all of a sudden
my Aunt Ethel shouts "Tonk!"
and slaps down her winning hand.
"Damn," my Aunt Maggie shouts.
"Damn," my Uncle Henry follows,
throwing his hand down in
disgust.
"Damn," my Uncle Leo echoes
as Aunt Ethel takes another
swig of her highball and with a
big grin on her face still flushed
with victory asks,
"Would anybody mind
if I deal the next hand?"

Funeral Laughter

At my grandmother's
funeral, two of my long-
lost cousins from Bow Junction,
Arkansas, walk into the services
ten minutes late and ask
my greatly bereaved uncle,
who took care of my grandmother
in the last years of her life,
"Is these seats tooken?"
Later my uncle,
retold the story his way—
"Could you believe it. I'm sitting there
thinking about my poor mother
laid out cold in the ground and
here come Filbert and Eloise, with
her big country-assed self,
wanting to know,
'Is these seats tooken?'
I thought, 'Well the blood of
Jesus, from what cotton patch
in Mississippi did these people
just walk out of?
Is these seats tooken?'
Lord have mercy."
In spite of the graveside service we
had to face in the morning,
we found ourselves unable to
control the uproarious laughter
that seemed to come from nowhere.
We stood
before the hot dishes and hams
people had brought
asking
over and over again, "Excuse me,
is these seats tooken?"

Akhenaten

I

I went there
to see her at the Robert Taylor Homes
on 35th Street and Federal.
It was like I'd
gone into a great earthen tomb—
all hollowed out, cool, dark, and foul smelling,
with glistening wet walls.
Sounds were sorrowful baritone,
baleful bass,
all brought low to the ground
scraping the bottom of the barrel:
desperate shouts and screams,
cries, followed by harsh
muffled laughter.
I timidly knocked on your door
and it opened
to your sad, dark, bug-torn eyes.
Enclosed within these tiny, concrete,
roach-infested rooms,
everything clogged for the afterworld:
old china,
a picture of Christ
over the old phonograph,
cheaply made French Provincial chairs
bought on time,
old magazines,
glass bowls,
goblets, dishes.
You smiled and simply
closed the door,
and we talked for hours
on your couch until dark;
and all that time,
I could only think about this

being one of my old recurring
nightmares
of Devil's Disciples,
Imperial Gangsters,
and Egyptian Lords,
and how would I get out
of here alive?
Then you calmly led me out
through the dark entryway
and in my behalf
appealed to those gangsters
who ran the building —
Tojo, Mikey, Casino.
You saying I was all right
because I was with you.
They were all waiting for something strange
to enter their own lives
and change them forever,
but they gave a nod —
I was a small fish.

II

Years later, my wife
and I sat on a grassy knoll for hours
in the sweltering July sun
with tourists from Iowa, New York,
and California,
all waiting for a chance to glimpse
antiquity thousands of
years old —
Anubis, lead us to Akhenaten,
Nefertiti. We enter the
cool hollow hallway of
the Museum of Natural
Science and History. Among
the gold and bronze statuettes,
I see beautifully carved *your* face again

as you led me out by the
hand, kissing me good-bye
lightly on my cheeks,
letting me come back from the underworld
into the world of the living again—
safe and unscathed
for that moment.
I promised to return,
all the time knowing
I wouldn't come back to see you
as I watched you that evening enter antiquity
through that small dark entryway,
your perfectly carved face set in
white alabaster against the light,
as you disappeared from this life forever.

My aunt,
a large, light tan
woman
drank a lot,
and called
her black
wire-framed brassiere
her "Titty Boat."
"Get me my Titty Boat"
she'd shout at me
from the bathroom.
And I would—
then I'd watch
in amazement from
a small crack in the door
as she slipped
her exotic cargo
deep into
its black holds.

A True Story

She came home early from work one morning
and found them in bed together.

Get outta here—
she tiptoed quietly back to the
kitchen and reheated the red beans and rice
she'd cooked for him the night before
Get outta here—
she came back to the bedroom and
waited until both of them were about
to reach the fateful moment together
Get outta here—
then just as they did, she poured
the whole pot of boiling hot beans
all over his bare ass
Get outta here—
then she calmly said to the woman
before she walked out of there for good,
"Baby, if you want to put some rice on top of that, you'll
have to go to the kitchen and get it yourself."
Get outta here—

"She didn't really say that to her, did she?"

When watching the classic thriller
Psycho more than thirty years ago
on the Southside
near my grandmother's two-bedroom
Ida B. Wells apartment,
the audience hooted as
Anthony Perkins
put the murdered woman's body—
carved up like a carrot—
into the trunk of the car,
considered the stack
of money she'd stolen,
put it into the trunk
with her body as well
and then heaved the whole
kit and caboodle into
the swampy quicksand.
As it sank,
a near riot commenced
in that dark theater.
People stood
in their seats shouting,
catcalling, shaking their fists
at the silver screen
as the car slowly sank
into the murky ooze.
A nattily dressed gentleman
in the third row
jumped to his feet
and shouted in vain
at the schizoid homicidal Bates,
"The money, fool, get the money
you stupid motherfucker!"
The tension broke and suddenly
everyone laughed
as he turned in half-mock

indignation and stormed up the aisle
heading out of the theater
before the movie was over
followed by the steady
applause of the audience
for his stellar,
once-in-a-lifetime performance.

In a cold school auditorium
I remember singing
"Lift every voice and sing."
Billy was farting blue
clouds through his thick baggy
corduroy pants. Jesse
whispered, "Gas attack, gas
attack," and pinched his
nose. Angela Jameson admonished
in a low voice, "You all stop
being so nasty!" Henry jumped
in saying, "That's what I told
yo' mama last night."
Howls and gales of laughter, bent
over, hands covered
mouths. Miss Weldon
cracked her baton,
"Now children, this is
our national anthem — show
some respect." We straightened
up: all dark-eyed souls chastened
to the serious nature of the
world outside. We take it
from, "sing a song full of
the hope that the future
will bring us."
Bill Foster lets a gigantic
"schzzoto." Henry jumps back,
"Oh, damn, man."
The choir dissolves into thick syrupy
laughter.
Miss Weldon jerks her
head around like a
startled, trapped doe, red rising on
her leather tan face. "What's so
funny about this song," she asks

as we try to straighten up.
"Tell me, what's so funny
about what Negroes had
to put up with in
this country for two
hundred years."
We were stiff and straight
as boards. We looked
ahead stony faced, serious:
the years starting to already mark
our features. "Now," Miss Weldon
said raising her baton,
"That's much better.
Let's take it from
'Sing a song full of the
hope that is in us.'"
And then we lifted our voices and we sang it
in a straight-faced way—
with somber-toned seriousness,
without "all this foolishness"
as Miss Weldon would say.
As Henry turned to me and gave me
a knowing wink, a thumbtack between his fingers
gliding directly
toward Angela Jameson's large and
already womanly behind—
waiting for just the right
moment for the final chorus of
"Lift Every Voice" to begin.

Aunt Janey's Great Northerns and Bacon Fat

Aunt Janey could
hear the
snap, crackle, and pop
of Uncle Buford's slow jazz song.
Are the kids outside?
Way outside.
Is the door locked?
Twice.
He continued his solo;
not so loud,
she said.
Look who's talking,
Miss Please-Lord-Please-Lord-
Oh-God-
Heavenly-Father *herself.*
Well, they think
I'm up here praying,
and I told them
I have to sometime shout out
His name to get His attention
way up there in heaven.
She stuck her head up from the pillow
and sniffled the air.
Smells like your beans
are burning; have you got the
gas on too high?
Naw, he said, I just gotta go down
there and stir them a little
with this big ol' paddle.
Well, I'll shut up then
so you can go down and get to stirrin' them.
Yeah, you shut up for the time being anyway,
he said, leaning down on his elbow.
What do you mean for the time bein'?
Until you get to praying, again.
Buford.

What?
You shut up yourself!
Stir them beans so they don't
get burned on the bottom.
Yes, Ma'am, I got the paddle
right here.
Suddenly the whole house was filled
with the warm and intimate smell
of great northerns simmering in
smoked ham hocks
and sizzling bacon grease.

Aunt Janey Visited by the Spirit

It was a hot
Sunday morning
at the First Ebenezer
Baptist Church on the Southside of Chicago
and the paper fans flicked
and flittered in the pews like
giant white butterflies
emblazoned
with a picture of a
praying, belighted Jesus
painted on their broad wings.
The preacher was elevated far above us
and tolled his voice
like a bell against
the thick hard surface
of our song. Every word
he spoke, a clap of thunder
was heard—to the beat—
like Catholic bells down the street
atop the great gothic cathedral
rung incandescent by a ringer gone mad
by the wound of his own ringing.
Over and over again
he dredged up the old
familiar crimes that
we stood convicted of
long ago: Adam and Eve,
Cain and Abel, Sampson and Delilah,
David and Bathsheba.
We were them and they were us.
The church
rocked and swayed
like Noah's Ark
as outside the storm raged
and the world,
the preacher exhorted,

went to
hell in a handbasket.
I looked at Janey.
This great, powerful,
dark chocolate brown woman
turned to a "a pillar of salt"
by his words,
as tears welled in her eyes
and rolled down her cheeks—
taking a mountainside's
worth of rouge and mascara
avalanching down with them.
She suddenly threw up her
arms in the air, stood up
and shouted, "Lord help me!"
Then, like a great
sycamore felled by
one blow of a sharp mythical ax,
she toppled straight back
into the hard pew.
Organ music seemed to commence on cue
along with scattered
"Amens!" and, "Yes, Lord!
He's certainly with us now!"
Women dressed in white
nurse's uniforms swept
in on both sides
fanning Janey and
trying to lift her head to give her
room to breathe and a little
water to drink.
At that moment I almost
lost it when Janey's eyes
rolled far back
into her head and a faint moan
secreted from deep in
her throat. "She's dead!"
I shouted. The women
laughed at my panic.

"No, darling, she's just fallen out
because the spirit has visited her,
that's all." They started
to lift her up—she,
still ashen, moaning, eyes
closed—as the choir
broke into
"Heareth Thy Name."
Just as I thought
I felt the rush of the
spirit taking me also, I
saw Janey crook her head
toward me, open
one eye calmly, and whisper,
"Philip, don't leave my
red patent leather purse
lie there under the pew
where I dropped it."
Then Janey closed her
eye and let the women
in white lead her out
to the church infirmary
as I followed behind,
clutching
her red patent leather purse
in my arms.

Aunt Janey and the Blues

In the late sixties when I brought home my friend Mick, who was a hippie with shoulder-length hair, a Jesus-style goatee, bell-bottom pants, tie-dyed T-shirt and Hare Krishna bells around his ankles, Aunt Janey was momentarily stumped (stunned would be more appropriate) but she decided, in the true spirit of the sixties, to play along anyway. Mick was very excited to be on the black Southside, home of his boyhood heroes: Little Walter, Luther Allison, Buddy Guy and Junior Wells. To him, he was musically making hajj back to the origins of his faith, which was the blues. With all the enthusiasm of a blonde-haired, blue-eyed Park Forest College cheerleader leaping high in the air and doing leg splits, he pulled out his harmonica proudly and did his best Sonny Boy Williamson imitation. My Aunt Janey's partials almost dropped out of her mouth. Later, when Mick left, Aunt Janey gave me a thorough going over. "Where did that boy learn how to play that harmonica like that?" "Old records, I guess." "And that hair, he don't look like a speck of water has hit his body in at least a week. Is he a hillbilly or something?" "No, he lives in Wilmette and his father is head of some big bank downtown." "Lord, Lord, Lord, and to think that his parents let him run around the streets looking like that." Then she looked at me suspiciously, "I'd better not see you out there in the streets lookin' like something the cat drug in, embarrassing me and your mamma." "You don't have to worry." "It's enough that you listen to that ol' gut bucket music." "You mean the blues," I weakly reply. "What you talkin' about, boy," she said with stern authority but in almost a mock-chastising tone. "What do you and your little hippie boyfriend from Wilmette know about the blues?" "We're starting a band," I said sheepishly. "Band? To play what?" Hands on her wide hips grinning. "The *Blues?* Well," she threw her chest out, "have you heard of *these* blues?" and she sang just like I heard Bessie Smith sing it on the record:

> *I Got Grea-a-at Big Legs*
> *with Plenty Meat on the Bone*
> *and Everytime I shakes*
> *a Skinny Gal Lose Her Home.*

"No, I didn't think you'd heard of them blues. Now. Go tell Mick to get him a haircut and some decent clothes and a good job. Life ain't no game, let me tell you; 'cause the blues ain't nothin' but a low-down dirty shame!"

Aunt Janey and Mabel Cook Soul Food

Aunt Janey
cooks the
gray wrinkles in
a big cast-iron kettle
and tells me
how once one of
her "liberal white friends"
invited her to dinner
and with an aim to please,
cooked "soul food."
She had everything laid
out—greens, okra, ham, and fried chicken—
it was all fine till she brought out the chitterlings.
"I said, 'Mabel, baby, did you make these all by yourself?'
She smiled a proud-as-punch,
cat-ate-the-canary smile
and said, 'Yes, indeed.
Let them thaw, boiled
them like you said you did
with onion.'"
Janey said she looked
down at the pot of steaming
hog intestines, started to
fork through it, and pulled
a wad of straw up.
Mabel screamed.
"Did you clean these before
you cooked them?" Janey asked.
Mabel looked puzzled,
"Clean them?"
"Yeah," Janey continued as she
forked up more straw.
"We want to eat the pig,
darling, not
what the pig ate."
"Oh," Mabel said and took

the pot back to the kitchen
chastened and a little embarrassed,
yet undaunted—"Yeah?" I said.
"Yeah," Janey said, "because
then she comes out with a big plate
of pig knuckles.
I asked her right up front,
'Mabel, did you
boil and pickle
them feet?'
'Boil and pickle them?' she said."

Aunt Janey Meets Sister Caudhill

Aunt Janey would buy her hats from Sister Caudhill, the hat lady, who would sell from door to door. My aunt was one of her loyal and regular customers. Janey would quickly pick out her Sunday-go-to-meeting wide-brim bonnet, felt or straw, depending on the season, and then sit back for the real stuff to commence. That would be the stories Sister Caudhill would regale my aunt with about her days as a madam of one of the most popular whorehouses on the Southside of Chicago. "Janey, darlin', I'll tell you one thing. All the men be they black or white would want the same thing. If he was white, you'd know for sure he'd pick out the bluest, blackest thing there, and if he was a colored, he wanted the whitest, blondest funeral parlor pale girl we had available. I don't know what it was—but each wanted the different race. Asked for it and paid for it too!" Mrs. Caudhill would sit back and ponder for a while. "I could never figure it." "What?" Janey asked. "Why they never ask for one of their own kind." Janey blew a wise whistle and quipped, "Oh, Sister Caudhill, maybe they just figure they could get one of their own kind any ol' time of the day. So they willin' to pay for something different and in their minds—special makes it something." "Ain't that the truth." Sister Caudhill gave a wink and knowing laugh upon which Janey smoothed her dress out, cleared her throat and in much indignation answered, "Well, ya know I'm a Christian woman now and wouldn't know anything about such goings on." Upon which Mrs. Caudhill snorted, "Well, I would say you know quite a bit already to still be a Christian woman and all." Janey laughed, "I'll say a big Amen to *that*, Sister Caudhill. Now, take that yellow straw hat with the blue feather tail out of the box while you at it!"

Aunt Janey Restin' Her Eyes Some

I remember how she'd
sleep so deeply, so soundly,
it was as though she were already
dead and laid out in her
smooth mahogany casket,
stony still, her dark brown face perfectly
made up, hair done, and in
her best Sunday-go-to-meeting
dress. I would suddenly run to her in a panic
and shake her hard awake.
"What's wrong, baby?" she'd say, startled.
"What's the matter?"
Then she'd look at
the old terror in my face and
she'd smile and hold me close to her
and say, "Don't worry none, I wasn't
really 'sleep,
I was just restin' my eyes some."

Serious Drinking

Up to six beers,
his absolute limit, he
thought of his dad
long in the grave from drink.
Pounding down six Budweisers
on the old man's off-day was just like
a starting pitcher warming up in the bullpen.
He remembered
Uncle Alvin who'd come
in with a quart of
Beefeater's and club soda; he'd
sweep away the dozen or so
cans of empty Miller High Life
with one arm and announce,
"It's time to bend the elbow,
get down to
some serious drinking."
The morning
after their highball card-shark night was
always cloudy: gray-streaked clouds over
the kitchen sink, gray cirrus clouds
in the chest of drawers,
gray cumulus clouds under the brass beds.
The single fact of the world was suddenly
film-documentary-gray, as gray as old
Aunt Lil shuffling
through gray dawn
to make milky gray coffee,
talking gray words that
stuck to the end of her
thick, chalky-gray tongue
that filled the empty gin
bottles and cocktail glasses
with gray ashy chinks
as the grayest two-fisted snores
arose from my aunts and uncles

sleeping in the next room
and hung over the house
like the long gray hair
of the dog.

The First Christmas After Their Divorce

Coming home
for Christmas
after their divorce,
though it wasn't
final yet—as if anything
really is—
I could have died
to see my mother's
things taken away
and in their place
a space as empty
and windy as any
western plain.
My father tried
to make small talk
but that didn't
go far. It started to
snow, so we went out
to buy a tree and
brought it back
and decorated it.
I remember the
red, green, yellow, and
blue lights, how
they once enthralled
me in the middle
of the night as my
sister and I woke and
tiptoed into the
living room.
The presents
arranged under the tree
shone like smooth rocks
under a clear stream.
Now my father
shrugs it off,

makes light of it,
but the dark spaces
grow under the
branches that flex to
the breaking point
with tinsel and ornaments
my mother,
in her haste to leave,
didn't bother to take.

Children of Ham

Suddenly I can hear
the Buddha, the Compassionate
One. My grandfather
standing on the back porch
lecturing my father
through the window I just broke,
my father's fists balled burgundy red
like overripe grapes.
"Don't beat the boy, James.
He told the truth.
He didn't mean it."

So what's with this curse?
Twenty-nine years later
walking down Jeffry Boulevard
I see a girl of seventeen:
her thin, wobbly
brown frame bending to
pull the cord on some
scarecrow toddlers of hers;
one shadow trails in the dust
almost a block away,
close to the onrush of cars,
the other shadow far beyond
as if running away from her.

When you turn on a light
they suddenly scatter everywhere
under sinks, dishes, tables,
under boxes of corn flakes.
How did so many come in here?
She looks at me unbelieving of my words,
gets the Raid
and coolly sprays the whole kitchen
from corner to corner.

Mother, I was under the impression
that I wasn't like these people.
They were foreign, pent-up,
always on TV
on the edge of some terrible disaster.

Even though I must confess this came
close to home one afternoon when
I walked into my father's bedroom
without knocking. He was sleeping off
a drunk—naked except for his white
jockey shorts—on the side of the bed
a half-empty bottle of beer. In his left
hand, a lit cigarette burning down to his
bare knuckles and into the mattress.
Without a word, I flicked the cigarette
from his fingers and crushed it out
in an ashtray. There was a small burnhole
in the mattress. He woke and stared at me
in surprise. "What do you want now?"
Without a word,
I walked out of the room
and closed the door behind me.

Alyce Lorraine Hampton Bryant

Half-this, half-that,
racially "tan," she was often
with short natural hair
before it was called "natural,"
then "Afro" without explanation.
Mistaken for Ethiopian,
Egyptian, or Sudanese,
she was Leonard's only
daughter, raised a tomboy,
his center and ghostly other.
When he died
she cried like the
bereaved lover.
She came out
of a strictly human caste
or so she told her children;
told us
to think for ourselves—
not mere apostrophes of a
captive, despised race,
but larger than that
mere coincidence
of a natural fact.
She'd rewritten
the prepared script
of her own life—and then
rued the day,
since she'd been
"running buddies"
with Lorraine Hansberry.
She spun out other orbits
where we could create as well,
with our own going beyond
a single category
as the primary consideration.
She'd quote

Shakespeare and Rousseau,
yet the two were confused
in our minds—
distant contradictories.
Yes, a way to make anew,
yet a longing to be right here—
while in our darkening minds
we tended to those ever-present dangers.
We were captive
to her half-baked vision,
her rage so mired
with stately reference
to our true humanity.
Our own individuality
took us away from
the "what is"
that made our
physical features so
African-seeming,
feeling so like a sting
against the levelings of
freedom marches,
the cause,
the crusade.
To diffuse
her other worldly energies
that the unconscious
country at that time
would not accept,
she developed other
strategies:
block-club meetings,
church-women's proceedings,
demure political and social verities,
as well as a petition
to keep a bus terminal
from being built in our
stiff middle-class
neighborhood.

A real ball of wax
that deflected
and yet oddly defined
the real issue,
the singular cause
to pass on to us
in those overheated
sixties, a sense
that we weren't really
just "black"
but to her something
more than that,
and she, on the contrary,
took offense at this
newly arrived consciousness
and spoke not of "black"
but "Negro" history
as an almost-corrective
for those then shark-infested waters.
The riots were her plum
to eat with relish,
to prove
her own point,
about the pit buried deep
in the sweet flesh;
she cast empirically based
judgments upon this
seemingly new
emerging race:
"The more things change,
the more they remain the same."
She was resigned
as the whole West Side of Chicago
burned
and Fred Hampton lay
in a bullet-riddled heap
on his bed.
She offered me
better advice,

more down-to-earth
common sense,
as a matter of personal survival
in those troubled times.
"Think not of yourself as
educated, sensitive, cultivated—
if you join the
rabble and a white policeman
sees you,
none of these things count.
To him you're just a nigger."
So the answer for her
was to finally withdraw
and quietly build her
own domain: make it
invisible as well as intractable
should anyone unworthy
try to enter and face the loneliness
of a truly lost cause—
as she did herself,
dying of cancer
just after turning fifty.
In her bed,
obstinate, taciturn
still, in her own words,
"self-reliant,"
her whispering deflated voice
over the phone telling me,
her only son, "I'm not dying.
Cancer's a doctor's hoax.
It's a question
of mind over matter;
don't rush here for me,
I'll beat the crab,
I'll make it through, you'll see."
But the "what is"
finally had its day,
and later my sister bitterly
turned to me

and said, "I saw her dying
into a heap of skin and bones;
you should have never believed
her, you should've been there."
Forgive me, Shaun,
for abandoning you.
What you say is true.
But as her only son,
in the end I
could have only done
what she wanted me to do.
It is the loneliness
of that senseless and unfounded
hope she spoke of
that I speak to now: for Clair,
for you.

The Sound of Their Laughter

People's laughter
that I grew up around
sounded like a
bucket of brown paint
falling from
a tall stepladder.
There was always
a sudden whoosh and thud
that cracked through
their lips, a moment
of silence inhaling
enough air,
as the splat of their overturned voices
spread quickly across
the seams
of bare, hardwood floors.

Stargazing

Aunt
Edith
was
shot
dead
during a
poker game
in her
Southside Chicago apartment.
My Uncle Charles
points to the pattern of
bullet holes in the walls
near the ceiling
like he's some
cockeyed farmer
from Kandiyohi
County
in central Minnesota
showing his
nephew
the constellation Orion
when in fact
he is pointing
to Ursa
the bear.

My Uncle Charles
solemnly told us
the news. Stalwart, Christian
Aunt Mary "had passed on."
"What?" I asked.
"She's gone to meet the Master,"
my uncle said quite regally.
"Where did she go to meet him?"
"Why, in heaven," he said, getting
a bit perturbed at my insisting.
"Why did she want to meet him?"
"He called her," he said,
getting a bit impatient now.
"Well, what'd He call her for?"
"Because," his voice starting to rise,
"one day He'll call us all."
"But why couldn't He just call her
on the telephone
and tell her what He wanted?
Why did she have to go to heaven
just to meet Him?"
Suddenly Uncle Charles stopped, got quiet,
staring a long time,
and finally said,
"Look, Philip, Mary's dead—*she died*—
stopped breathing," he took a deep sigh.
"Well, why didn't you say that
in the first place?" I said,
walking away indignant, confused.
Later, I'd try to picture the "Master"
of my biblical coloring book meeting
Aunt Mary with his long flowing
robes, beard and long hair,
sad eyes and outstretched hands,
but couldn't quite trace
the exact outlines of the figure
with my young hand.

Aunt Janey Speaks of the Crooked Preacher

Aunt Janey suddenly
remembered a notorious
Baptist preacher from long ago who
purportedly fleeced his flock
and fucked the fold as well.
She laughed,
"Yeah,
he was so crooked
that when he finally died,
they had to
screw him into the ground."

Soul Food

Yesterday's chit'lin's in the Frigidaire congeal miraculously into our one true faith.

Sweet potatoes, or candied sweets, taste like the water a boy swimming on his back suddenly swallows so that he has to flip over and do the Australian crawl.

My Uncle Richard devised the Archangel's cornbread and perfected it under fire in Korea. Drunk as a skunk back home, he held me in his arms for hours, stirring the ingredients of an epiphany.

Ham hocks were whale meat. I was an Eskimo home from the long hunt. Outside it was thirty below; inside, the meat of the walrus and seal, "ai-EEEEEEEE!" My father just sighed and shook his head at me from across the table.

Okra is not for the faint of heart—deep kissing or perilous sexual goo—"Stop it now," my cousin shouted, "or I'll tell," as I tried to put okra down her dress at Thanksgiving dinner.

Lake Superior white, catfish, or buffalo—breaded in a golden light cornmeal. The Holy Trinity of freshwater fish.

Black-eyed peas—like fat women, I didn't know then that I liked them so much or that they tasted so good.

Grits should come down like the Berlin Wall. They've been standing too long, creating a frozen and amorphous tundra between Saturday morning homemade buttermilk biscuits, sausages, and eggs. I quietly pushed them to one side of my plate and left them there like a pile of dirty snow melting in early spring.

Pig knuckles are like basement apartments: you live in them until times get better and then you move. You don't stay in them and try to make them your home.

Turnip greens, collards, and mustards—all should achieve sainthood in the next century.

A slab of barbeque ribs is like a camp-out without mosquitoes, flies, or ticks—no woods to get lost in; no search parties for weeks futilely beating the bushes for any traces of you.

Oxtails was the dish my father created for us instead of writing the great American novel or leaving us a million dollars in his will.

Deep fried chicken should be called from three times a day like the parapets in Istanbul, or it should be given out during Holy Communion.

Watermelon has no race, color, or creed. Its day-old rinds discarded in the garbage can treat every fly, no matter what its origin, equally.

Spaghetti—surprise! Not cooked "al dente"—forget it. You boil it for a week and then stir it up with a can of Delmonte tomato sauce and then let it simmer for a week more.

These are all essential dishes making complete the sacred rib and chit'lin' dinner that naturally fills the soul of man.

Looking for Her Body

From across the
street, almost a block or more
away, she's on her regular
walk, and I'm looking
for her body:
a tiny speck of something or other,
a blot on the blue horizon,
a blown cinder, a black bird,
a lost airplane, a snapped kite,
heading this way as now
I can make out the shape
of her well-built, stocky
closely-hugging-the-ground body;
her familiar
hazel-colored hair
cut shorter over the eyes,
then closer still until the facial
features are one after the other
perfectly visible.
Her cheekbones were raised
on some Indian reservation,
the eyebrows arranged
like furrows of wild grass
along some lonesome stretch
of highway, the slight dimple
above the chin is The Angry
Red Planet rising in the late
August sky. Then closer,
the neck with its fine line breaks
into the perfect poem we can
only dream of writing.
A few freckles dust the surface
of her bare skin in late March
early April—
then closer still,
the outline of her large hips—

those swing low sweet chariots
beneath her brown corduroy jeans.
Her smooth calves bristle as she steps,
her large rounded thighs
rub two great continental divides and
the friction naturally creates
a steep precipice that drops somewhere
off the cliff of buttocks —
billowing out like sails
that make a swishing sound of spray
hitting the sleek prow
somewhere out at sea.
Closer still, the
windless quiet nightfall of earlobes,
the hand and fingers
blowing gauzy white
from the open bedroom window,
I watch her walk away —
the small of her back moves
down the street like a
sparse quarter moon in January
setting under cold stiff poplars.
The elbows and soles of the feet
are tiny flickering lights of
late-night revelers
moving off to new stomping grounds;
and now at the farthest point where
I can only imagine her body,
there is a speck again as she
is far enough away so that I
can't tell if she's disappeared completely
or if she's turned around and is
walking back toward me again,
as I stand a little while longer
in the twilight looking for her body.

The Park Worker

The harbor is as a baby's blue eye
blinking through the sunlight.
The boats rest in their moorings
as a dredger brings up beer cans,
paper cups, and bottles filled with sand.
A young black girl working for the park
makes her way through the grass runway
spearing bits of paper, flicking them
into a green canvas bag slung over her back.
She is slow, halting, breathing deeply
as if every movement
takes almost her entire strength.
She stops to look at what remains of her
work—she has not even finished a fraction
of the runway that stretches
to the other end of the harbor.
A bright red Olds Cutlass drives by,
honks its horn.
She shouts something back at it, inaudible,
waving her hands high in the air,
back and forth, desperately,
as if trying to get the car to stop,
but it drives past and is soon
out of sight.
The girl stands there for a moment looking
out on the harbor, the midway stretching 'round—
its green and wet hem littered with refuse
of Sunday's picnics and barbecues—
and slowly, ever so slowly
she spears another piece of paper
and puts it into her green canvas bag
and moves down the incline toward the water.

Portrait of a Woman at the 7-11

She stands in the grocery line
stoop-shouldered,
haltered with slumbering
flesh accumulating
like deep drifts of snow
on the back porch stairs.
Her winter is now,
even in the middle
of July.
Her slow walk
from the bedroom
to the kitchen
in the early morning light
where she peers through
the open refrigerator,
thaws her.
Her husband's snores
resound through
prefab walls;
never wanting
the shade
of her slowly
bending body,
leaf after leaf
is lost to the autumn wind.

Polka Dancing Televised Live from Mankato on Saturday Night

A dairy farmer all the way from Albany, Minnesota
and his very fat wife
danced to the polka,
"She's Too Fat for Me"
laughing and singing along with
the words, holding each other tight.
He twirled her like she was
some willowy dark-eyed Russian ballerina,
singing into her ear
like a teenager in love
for the first time
in his life.
"You can have her,
I don't want her, she's too
fat for me, she's too fat for me,"
as he lifts her off her feet
high into the air
and sets her three-hundred-pound frame down
as lightly as
a newborn babe in her crib at night.
She throws her head back
tango style
and gives out a raucous
rose-between-the-teeth laugh
as he starts in on
another chorus of the
"She's Too Fat for Me Polka"
before giving her another
of his death-defying twirls.

Here Comes Another Red Poem

Red Candles—Smoky Red Lights
Dave Etter

A red-haired mother and her red-haired daughter
from Red Earth County,
each weighing about 250 pounds
in the red portion of the scale,
drive down the road
in their brand new red pickup
going into town to
the Red Owl to buy
red soda pop and red hot
barbecue potato chips and
then maybe stop
at the drugstore
for some ruby red lipstick,
dark red eyeliner and rosy red
blush—then over to
Target for red
stretch pedal pushers, red
tank tops, red panties and
brassieres—and then
back into the red truck for
a ride home into
the red evening sky—
wearing red sunglasses to keep the red
setting sun from
shining on their red sunburned faces
as they pull into the driveway
with the red night-light
left on over
the red garage door
that opens and then closes
on their red-letter day.

Eleven Short Scenes from My Life

1.

There, sick in my bed in early June, an
evening rain shower subsided. The clouds broke away,
the setting sun shone on my friends in the alley
below my window playing "invisible man" baseball.

2.

It was quiet in the afternoon, ivies growing on the
garage wall, I had a new pair of P.F. Flyers, and tried
to outrun a passing airplane flying the length of my
backyard.

3.

In a field on my wife's father's farm late in autumn,
the windblown clouds are white puffs low in
the sky; it is cool but warmer in the sun—we
are concealed by trees and rows of corn, the cool wind
feels good on our bare skin.

4.

It is early morning, the beginning of March. Frost
is on the grass, but the snow is completely gone. The sky
is clear and deep blue; I don't know spring is coming
because I am too young to know what season it is.

5.

Driving back from St. Peter to Paynesville in
Renée's old Dodge packed with our belongings, taking
Highway 22 through Litchfield. Late summer sky, the crickets
purr, the corn tall and slightly brown. The sun is
setting directly in our eyes even though we are just starting out.

6.

Late August, first of September, it is a dark, early morning.
Rain pelts the windows, my mother rouses us from bed. I was
dreaming about being safe and warm from the driving rain and wind
outside. Suddenly a crack—lightning and then thunder—
"It's time for school," she says.

7.

The clouds are gray and low this time. I am in love again, but
she doesn't love me, so I imagine that she does and walk down
the street talking very softly to her, the wind pressing against
my navy peacoat, a book of William Blake's *Prophecies* in my pocket.

8.

Black sky, a tornado cloud zips overhead, I run screaming in terror
to the basement. My sister stands at the top of the stairs
laughing at me.

9.

Eating ham and cheese sandwiches on soft hamburger
buns, my Grandmother Bryant and I sit in the upper deck
third base side in a sea of white faces that soon become
kind and friendly toward us. The White Sox beat the
Red Sox 2-1, but Ted Williams hits a home run in the
top of the eighth that reached the left center field
lower decks.

10.

Renée arrived from Paynesville. We walk around Ft. Sheridan
beach. She has grown dark brown with golden blonde hair that
hints autumnal red-orange as if she were on fire or burning
something inside her. I embrace her and feel the outer
warmth of her skin on mine. My jaws are fatigued
from smiling so much.

11.

Piled into my grandfather's '57 Olds 88, we drive down
Lake Shore Drive: I see Lake Michigan for the first time—
brilliantly blue, immense, appearing over a rise. It is
the only time in my life I have ever felt that things could go on
forever without ending.

In Late Fall

I get goose bumps
when I see that
woman's wide goose down hips;
if she comes any
closer, I
just might sprout wings
and fly south with her
for the winter.

Looking at Your Body

To Renée

As you walk
to the mirror
and drop the towel
to the floor,
the beads of water
still pock
your smooth white skin.
You look with disapproval—
almost chagrined.
You pat the womb-worn tummy,
the too-solid
widening of the flanks.
Suddenly,
the gentle dips and bends
of country culverts,
deep ditches filling
with spring rain
appear as your body
simply has shifted a little in time,
grown over in places
or filled in somewhere else.
Yet, standing before you
I look at your body
for the first time as
in that field of ripe October corn
west of your parents' house.
Dusk, stretched out
naked as a jaybird,
we followed the rows
ear to ear
into the darkening west,
two limbs of a
windblown poplar
bent down
to finally embrace.

A Single Iris

For Renée

The iris
in your voice
tiptoed
to the edge
of the bed,
breathed in
the violet air,
peeled off the
outer garment of
a single petal
and stood naked in the moonlight.
A stark white
pungent bloom
appeared
and suddenly plunged
into the black smoked
glass vase
of night.
The stem—
surrounded
by a wild thrashing
ocean.
Your voice now comes up
from the water, a small white
sail on the very tip
of an enormous wave
crashing downward.

Riding Back on a Thirty-Year-Old Tractor After Pulling Out the Car I Drove into a Ditch, Watching Stars and Lightning from the Northwest

For Warren Reeck

Silent philosophy,
you and me
touching in the dark
like two shadows married to each other.
The noise of the tractor's engine
drowns out the dishonesty of our words,
the sky illuminates our faces into one vision:
the moment has arrived.
The tractor is moving down the road
at a speed we can both understand.
We join hands
through the night like
invisible brothers,
twins with the same mother,
the same god,
the same body;
and it's because we drive down this dirt
road together.
It is because the lightning flashes through
the black skin of the night,
lighting the way before us.
It is because the rocks that have grown
between us
have suddenly turned to stars and have sunken into
our bodies
sending a heat welding our joy together
like two roots joining the earth.
There is nothing to keep us apart,
not tonight; we will ride this tractor
home.

The snow blew
blue snowflakes
in Blue Island.
There was plump, jolly Judy Stanisloski
who bravely invited me out to her
house because somehow she
dug Horace, Sonny, and Miles
and knew I'd come.
She wrote her own little
verse in between
the tin frame houses,
blast furnace smokestacks
and goulash restaurants
of her girlhood—Blue Island.
She wanted to be another Emily Dickinson, I think.
I was the intrepid Columbus—
willing to take on
hostile, white, bone-through-their-noses tribes—
and risk life and limb
against Dago greasers, Polack bikers, Bohunk shop rats,
all dressed in white socks,
tight black Levi jeans and
black workshoes. Tangled in Chicago
"dees" and "dooes,"
the *Dems* were on the outs—
and didn't appreciate my little
biracial intrusion into their quiet
but unbelievable demise.
I called in the snow-blue
hours with piles of Miles,
Monk, and of course, Horace underarm.
We wiled away the afternoon
so blue in our funk
that it lost all its blueness
as she spoke of the blue mist
of her years. Ahead,

the human layaway plan of her life:
a life-sentence job at Ford,
cracker box brick bungalow,
punching metal frames,
and thousands of kids
waiting for her at home
to suck the fruit dry
of anything that was leftover
from the sparks and the welding machines
she OK'd. "Why would Negroes
ever want to integrate such
a hellhole like this anyway?
We're just a bunch of losers
way back from the last war."
Then we listened to Miles
and she got sweet and
brushed a good-bye kiss on my cheek.
We're going down two different tracks,
glad to at least meet at this station.
"Be seeing you. . . ."
Down the ice-blue streets I went.
The signs said it all,
"Niggers Beware," just below,
"Love, the KKK."
As factory smoke blew into the
blue snowflake sky
that lowered on
the small snow-blue
yards of Blue Island.

The Glue that Held Everything Together

We were all
stuck to the same
glue in 1967,
sticky as a roll of flypaper
and we didn't know it yet. To us,
our world was coming
up roses—Chicago Vocational
had just won the public league football
championship with big Polacks from Hegewisch,
Bohunks from Blue Island,
and swift-footed
colored boys from the Southside,
and we were all shit and grit in our shops
pinging and panging
the industrial rag
that would send us
either to the blast furnaces
of Gary or Vietnam.
For some, it was
their salad days:
hair greased back
Dago style, tight black
Levi jeans, and a cigarette
dangling like a crucifix
from their mouths.
No one would tell us
we were stuck
on this desert island
for the rest of our lives
and there wasn't no use
in trying to get out either.
So, we buzzed over our
souped-up cars
and looked forward to
annual three-percent raises.
The tiny, ramshackle bungalows

were built below
the smoking mills that called
us even then—as we
stretched out our wings
on Saturday nights
to impress our girls,
as fledglings often do, as if to fly
off with them somewhere;
but the glue that held
everything together back then
hardened fast as cement—
we flapped and flapped
but our wings got us nowhere.

Will the Last Person to Leave Please Turn Out the Lights

I went to the last
house on the left,
up to her apartment,
knocked on the last
door at the end of the hall.
It was the last day
of fall—one of the
last nice days before
the winter snow and bitter
cold set in. She said
she was sorry—it was the
last time she could see
me and gave
me one last kiss and hug.
We listened to
one of the last songs
Billie Holiday ever recorded
and danced one last
dance together and drank one
last drink until the
last of the wine was gone.
Afterward, on my
way out, I went down
the stairs
glancing back at her one last time
before catching the
last train
back to the city. By the time it arrived,
I was the last passenger
left in the car.
I ran to make
the last bus to the
Southside, filled
with tired, sad-looking people
just gotten off from
the last shift at the factory.

As we all rode, bumped
and tossed like rag dolls,
all of us looking like
the last dog hung
or the last die-hard fans at
the last baseball game of the year:
lost, during the very last at bat,
by a team
that manages to finish the year
dead last.

Early Inheritance

Now I play Ben Webster with Gerry Mulligan, the album cover's a fake fifties abstract expressionist painting, the album sleeve cracked open like a hayseed, which I taped closed later. All of them are a bit frayed and faded as I flip-flip-flip and find another Lester Young or Coleman Hawkins. Some, with his name written on the side, James Bryant—then ✳✳✳✳! (Four Stars!) He really liked it—maybe even loved it. It kept him company like his bottle, tuning out my mother's tirades as everything around us crumbled. So goes another civilization—Pompeii went in a day—so they say. My mother finally walked out my sophomore year of college. Like Vesuvius, she blew her stack, went through the roof and never came back. My dad was left with the remains—and precious gems scattered in between—I mean these records that he collected from the rubble. As one day, in a big display of grandstanding or bluster, he brought his whole collection and hi-fi equipment and dumped them into my room. I was fourteen at the time. "I'm sick of your mother's bitching," he'd said, "here's your early inheritance." He stalked out and I waited until the air was clear and while he slept, spirited back his records and hi-fi to their rightful place. He didn't say a word about it the next day, nor did I. I knew that I would be probably flipping through them one day after he died—Prez, Bird, Coltrane, Ellington. No tears now I said to myself; I must be as cold and full of purpose as an archeologist: sort, label, and catalogue for the archives. He would have wanted it that way. Just a clean transfer, no glitches or worn-out clichés. Just preserve the records I have in my possession for now, until one day when I'm too old, I suppose, I too, will have to let them go or give them away.

Locomotion

I heard the
locomotion behind
the album by Monk my father
was playing.
The finely tuned
machine humming like
a top, purring like a kitten.

The first time I
saw the Santa Fe "Super Chief"
at Union Station in Chicago,
gleaming as a silver bullet
carrying the blue uniformed
conductor who gave a low whistle
and "All Aboard" for places as far away as Kansas,
Laredo, Tucson, Las Vegas, Palm Springs.

At that point
I knew it all had
something to do with jazz music.
The slow hiss of
the engine, the steam
let out by the jowls of the locomotive,
and the massive, muscular wheels turning
slowly counterclockwise to the engine's beat

Come on Baby Do the Locomotion
Come on Baby Do the Locomotion With Me

heading out onto the open tracks,
that smoke-blown phrase repeated
over and over in my head through the years,
as miles of the real American landscape
began, slowly, to unfold.

The Island

Here the island is complete. The edges of the hard brick buildings are lapping against the shores: smoke billows instead of rain-laden tropical clouds. Beyond the narrow strips of beached pavement, an impenetrable darkness exhumes the birdlike call of the phonograph. The music rises like some Floridian tropical bird cawing from a twisted human-shaped limb. It was years before I noticed my street, Prairie Avenue, was an island. The music always seemed as natural as birds placed a million years ago after the last great volcanic eruption. But today, the way they picture the Southside, it was nothing of the kind. It wasn't a sort of carnival of clones—a voice dressed in anonymity and sameness: one arm stretched out from the bedside and we *all* stretched and gave a little spiritual rendition of, "It's a Great Gettin' Up Morning," a thick, glucosed gospel that cracked in our throats like a dozen eggs dropped from a grocery cart. But there *was* a brown and tan broom that swept the corner clean so that the peculiar edges would not show when company finally arrived.

Yet, I don't think about it until now. How the wind must have sounded to my father as it swept down the long coils of streets. The air was penitent and judgmental, the trees onerously green; one false step and you were enveloped in a green hazy light; the history left you alone to drink, rail, and play jazz records.

Minutia is important and detail is strung like microbes making the whole picture lifelike and real. The accumulating books and records, along with old magazines, stacks of unopened mail, empty cans of Schlitz Malt Liquor, old photos of Alyce and the kids—in those lonely, perfect days when promise spoke for all things, even when later it was found not to speak at all. You stood next to the doorway still young and slender, shy, smiling, yet distant, like a man dying of a rare disease that makes him appear normal and healthy all of his life until one day it kills him suddenly for seemingly no reason.

How much of an island was it? How did he make the dark lapping sound of automobiles and buses completely encircle the house like dark, entrenching waters? He drank, lit cigarette after cigarette in the dark. He played jazz record after jazz record and collected other people's garbage for a living. I always felt my own childhood came at the beginning of time when there were few people he could talk to about the marvelous inventions that would come later like the airplane, telecommunications, and open heart surgery. There was always a murky newness to the world. And the island took on a prehistoric red-orange hue at dusk. The birds would chirp as jazz played in the smoky reaches somewhere. And he seemed to be carrying on a conversation with someone like himself not yet born: someone who would evolve slowly and surely out of this primordial ooze of an island. He seemed to know even then that this was only 1958 and there was still a little hope lingering in a time well after his death.

Stella by Starlight

My mother couldn't understand how my father, a man stuffed so full of promise and potential, could wither it all away on a stack of bebop records and a bottle of beer. And his close friend, Preston, was worse—undereducated and couldn't speak the King's English if you'd held a gun to his head, gave him the book, and asked him to quote any passage out of Shakespeare. Every other word was *muthafuck* this or *muthafuck* that. Why my father associated with him, who in my mother's opinion was far beneath him, was an open mystery, something beyond her. Jazz, Jazz, Jazz, that's all she heard—*morning*, *noon*, and *night*—when he could have easily risen to be a great surgeon, lawyer, or civil rights leader. But one day I walked in on them by accident and there they were: Preston and my dad, a little drunk, crouched over the turntable. I understood why when they turned around, taken completely by surprise for an instant. I saw that both their dark faces reflected the light and were shining.

Gray Strands of Hair

To Renée

It's a
poor excuse
for a
violin string.
If you
stretch it
that far,
it would break
in two
without even
a popping
sound.
When you comb it out
and then, later
in bed,
when I touch
a gray strand
in the dark,
it suddenly crackles.
"Electricity,"
you say
nonchalantly,
as it throws off
little sparks
between us —
still,
after some
twenty-odd
years together.

Picking Wild Flowers

I have been out picking
wild flowers and some weeds,
if you like, that look like them—
"them" being a bouquet
laced with this or that
kind of flower.
I don't know which.
Can you look it up
in your book, later?
You look at me uneasily
because I smell
of a strange perfume
and my mouth is shadowed
as if by a kiss,
and you ask, was it just
for me that you went
and for so long stayed away?
I cannot answer
your question straight,
or otherwise; it's a fact
that I've been gone and have
now returned smelling of
different perfumes gathered
in this wild bouquet
but can't think of which
flower's name is which;
I just picked them randomly
without a thought.
They are all beautiful
and meant just for you;
I'm sorry it took so long.
You must have thought,
if he's taken this long,
it must be for someone else
he went.
Well, I can't say that—

or name one of these flowers
I just picked,
but believe me, this
time I gathered them
not knowing
or caring
what they were.
They were all beautiful
and meant for you,
so maybe later you
can look them up
in your book
to see what they are—
so this time we can
know their true names.

Ottawa, MN, Cemetery—1992

In memory of Otto Spavek

I

A million years ago
all these white people weren't even born
only this
layer of soft clay
like the clouds that now
quietly roll
over the lush green hills of
the Ottawa, Minnesota, cemetery.

II

Otto Spavek
Born 1892 Prussia
Died 1957 Ottawa, MN
Survived by his wife
Amelia and his daughters
Gretchen and Ruth, grandsons Otto II and Wilhelm—
and now Phil Bryant,
who traveled this lonesome road to southern Minnesota
all the way from
the Southside of Chicago.

III

Otto Spavek, you probably knew nothing about slavery, Jim Crow,
the W.E.B. Dubois and Booker T. Washington debate, Fred Douglass,
Nat Turner, jazz, blues, or gospel, Civil Rights or Black Power. In
turn, I know nothing about howling blizzards and killer ice storms,
diphtheria, failed crops, farm foreclosure, loneliness and death on
the prairie.

IV

Otto Spavek, I'm thinking about you
exactly a hundred years after your birth.
I, a black man born in the City of Big Shoulders
a long way from here,
seven years before your death.
Standing here beside your grave,
in the grand scheme of the universe,
it's like we missed each other by just minutes
on the express train of American history.
The crows perched high atop the dead cottonwoods
unfurl their black wings like they have for a thousand years or so and
seem to squawk at the thought of it.

Poetry

For John Calvin Rezmerski

Nowadays
poetry is created
by gathering statistics
on some theoretical vernacular and
then multiplying the number
of dissertations on the subject
by the number of literary critics
it takes to screw a light
bulb in a socket.
I still believe
a word should come
off the tongue
smelling like it was
just pushed out
of the womb,
screaming, kicking,
fitful and surly.
No shrinking violet here—
thank you,
or politely served
gin and tonics on a silver tray;
it should be 100 proof—
straight, no chaser.
This is our only hope,
to cradle this
hapless, hungry thing;
feed it, nurture it,
and finally
give it a name.

Acknowledgments

Philip Bryant was born in Chicago in 1951, educated in the Chicago Public Schools, and graduated from Chicago Vocational High School in 1969. He attended Gustavus Adolphus College and graduated with a BA in English in 1973. He attended Columbia University, School of the Arts, graduating with an MFA in creative writing in 1975. From 1975 to 1989, he taught at various colleges and universities in the Chicago area; among them were Chicago State University and Harold Washington College, City Colleges of Chicago. From 1989 to the present he has taught at Gustavus Adolphus College, where is currently an Associate Professor of English. He was a 1992 fellow of the Minnesota State Arts Board, and has served on the governing board of The Loft, the center for writing and creative arts located in the Twin Cities. He has had his poems published in *The Iowa Review*, *The Indiana Review*, *The American Poetry Review*, and *Nimrod*. *Blue Island*, a chapbook of his poetry, was published in 1997 by Cross+Roads Press.

He is also an avid student of jazz and has had his poetry set to jazz forms by Carolyn Wilkins, pianist, singer, and composer. Together they have put together a program of poetry and jazz honoring their Chicago roots entitled *South Side Suite*. He is married with three children and lives in Saint Peter, Minnesota.